A LITTLE OWL BOOK

1 2 3

written by Brenda Apsley
Illustrated by John Millington

WORLD

1

one old owl

2 two tired tigers

1

3

three thirsty thrushes

4

four fat firemen

5

five funny faces

6

six slow snails

7

seven striped socks

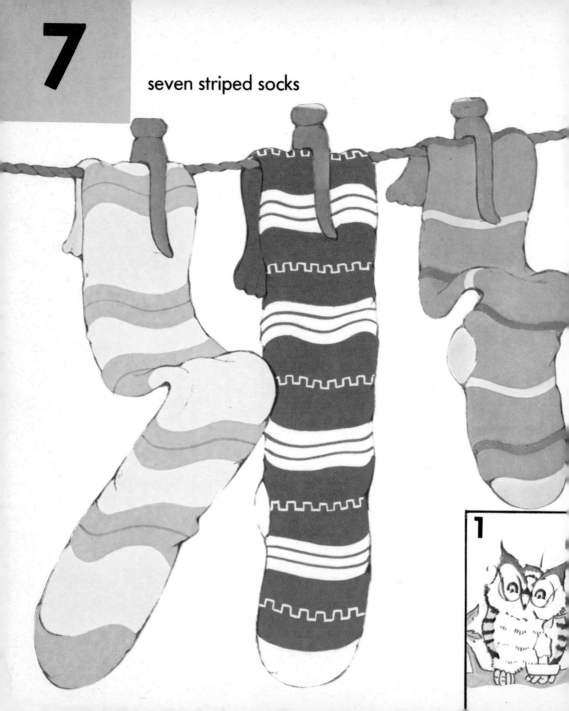

1

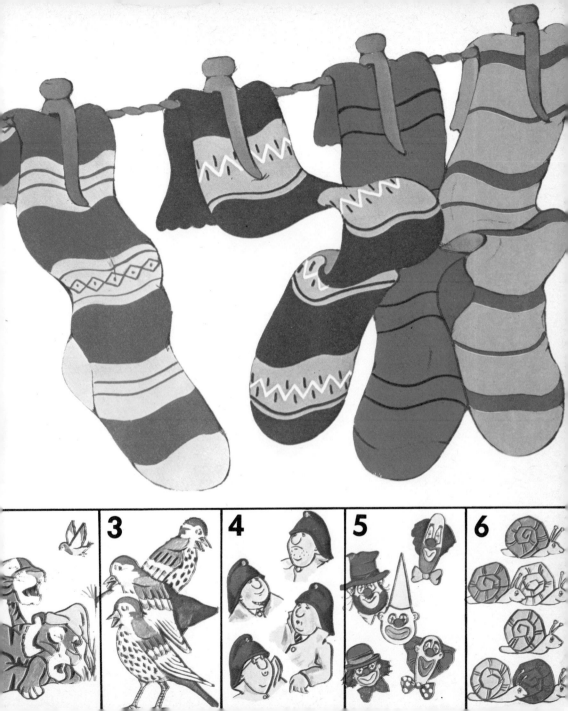

8

eight easter eggs

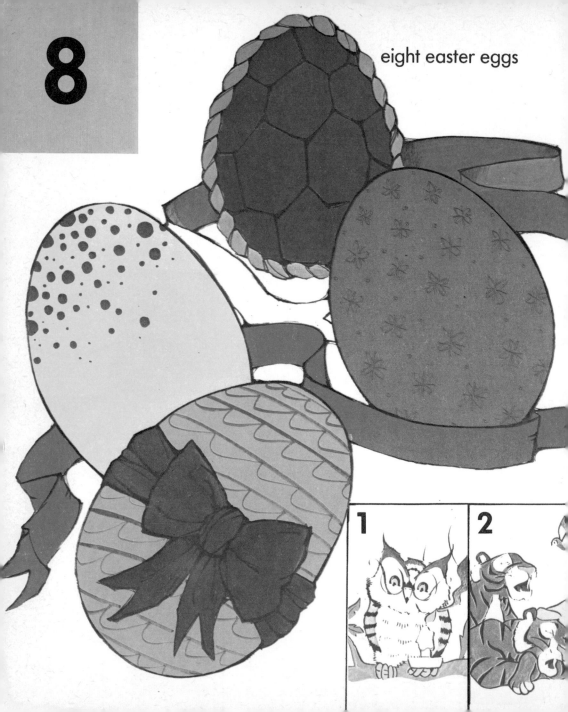

1

2

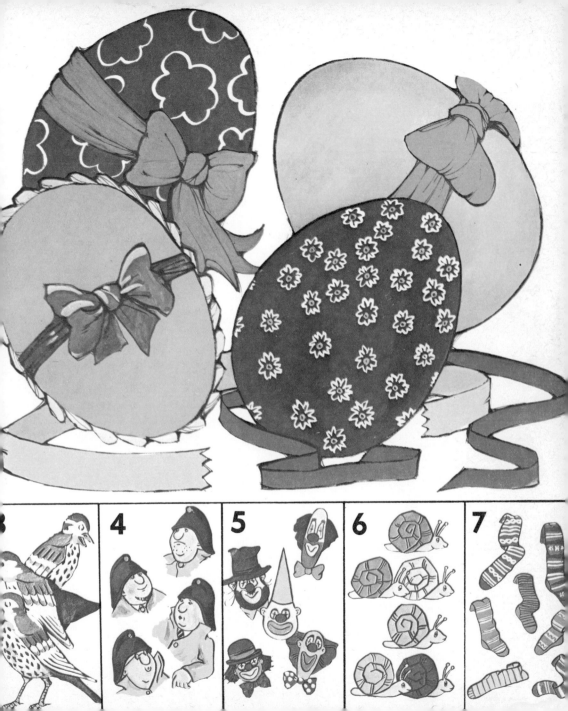

4

5

6

7

9

nine neat nurses

1 **2** **3**

10

ten tiny tadpoles

1 **2** **3** **4**

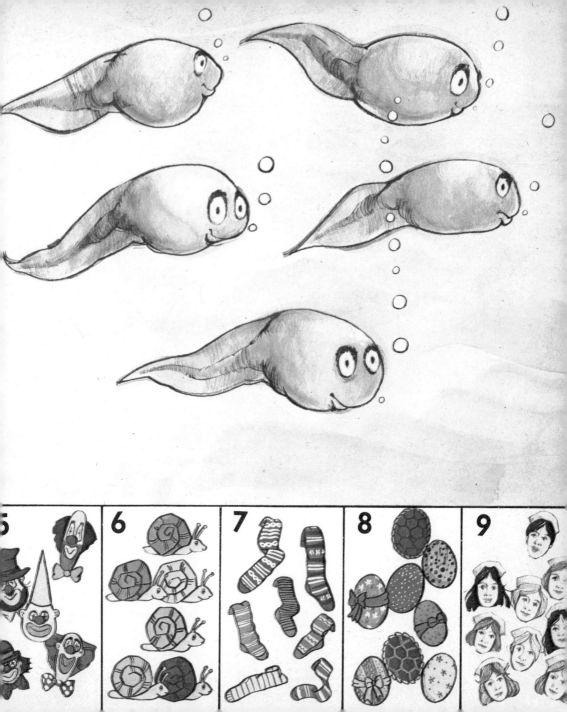

how many mice,
four, five or three?
let's count and see!

how many mice can you count?

how many birds on the washing line?
count them all – seven, eight or nine?

how many birds did you count?

how many skittles?

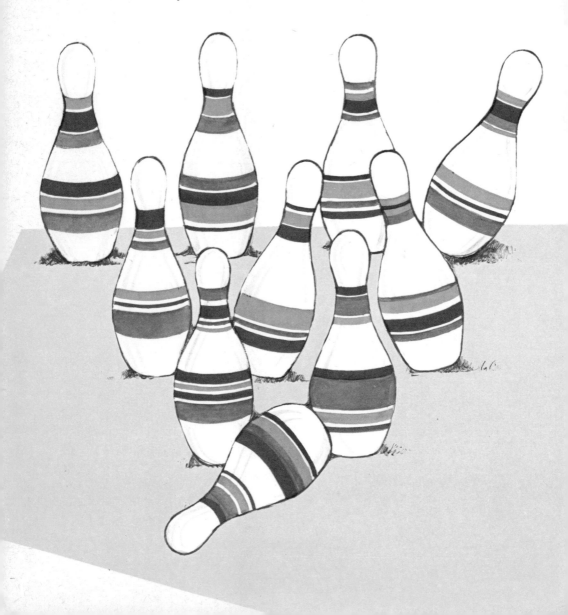

and how many balls?

how many triangles?
how many squares?